MW01127056

SCIENTOLOGY:

THE CULT OF GREED

SCIENTOLOGY:

THE CULT OF GREED

JON ATACK

Copyright © 2014 by Trentvalley ltd
Published by Richard Woods
All rights reserved.

This book is based on a talk given at the Alexander Nevsky Lavra, in St Petersburg, on 18 September 2014, on the anniversary of the death of James Marshall Hendrix, to whose memory it is dedicated.

CONTENTS

THE UFO CULT

Seventy-five million years ago, the evil Prince Xenu rounded up the populations of 76 planets and brought them to Earth, where their souls were dropped into volcanoes, blown up with hydrogen bombs and gathered on electronic ribbons to be clustered together.

This sounds like the creation of a science-fiction writer - and it is - but Scientologists who have reached the secret OT III level are told that they can only regain their individuality by separating themselves out from these impacted clusters of souls. And they pay tens of thousands of dollars to practice this contemporary form of demon exorcism.[1]

Scientology's creator, Ron Hubbard, claimed that anyone exposed to the secrets of this level unprepared would die within days, but, in the 1980s, he tried to sell a screenplay of the story, under the title *Revolt in the Stars*.

HARD SELL

The "Governing Policy" of Scientology, as stated by its creator, is to "make money, make more money" and "make other people produce so as to make money."[2] Scientology sales staff are trained extensively in hard-selling techniques, and have no compunction in pushing followers into remortgaging their houses to pay for Scientology courses. Many former members can testify that they were financially ruined by their involvement with Scientology. Recently, the cult has declared assets of four billion dollars to the American tax authorities. It is believed that it holds about the same amount outside the US, yet members of the core Sea Organization work a 90-hour week for a few dollars, surviving on substandard food, in over-crowded lodgings.

Hubbard said this of his Scientology courses: "Advanced Courses are the most valuable service on the planet. Life insurance, houses, cars, stocks, bonds, college savings, all are transitory and impermanent ... Advanced Courses ... last forever and give immortality. There is nothing to compare with Advanced Courses. They are infinitely valuable and transcend time itself."[3]

In a dispatch called "What is Life Worth? - The Importance of Hard Sell", Hubbard said, "HARD SELL is ... a MUST in dissemination and selling of services and materials."[4] In another dispatch, he says, of hard selling, "You tell him that he is going to sign up right now and he is going to take it right now ... One does not describe something, one commands something. You will find that a lot of people are in a more or less hypnotic daze ... and they respond to direct commands in literature and ads. Hard Sell means insistence that people buy."[5]

Hubbard made his notions clear in this passage: "NEVER let anyone simply walk out ... And never let a student leave or quit - introvert him like a bullet."[6] Further, "You have to be willing to invade privacy, very definitely ... [recruits] don't have any rights!"[7] In internal issues, Hubbard derided non-members as "wogs" - an English racist term - and called them "dead in the head"[8] and "raw meat."[9]

It has often been asserted that Scientology and Dianetics are hypnotic in nature. Hubbard made his own point on this subject: "You can control men like you would control robots with those techniques ... we've got some new ways to make slaves here."[10]

Although Hubbard claimed that he took nothing from Scientology - "the fees you pay for service do not go to me"[11] - by the time he died, he had accumulated $648 million. Scientology had long been his only significant source of income. The US Internal Revenue Service achieved judgments against Scientology, clearly showing that funds inured to Hubbard from the cult. Given this evidence, it is hard to think of Scientology as anything more than a moneymaking scam, but there is far more to this story.

In 1993, the cult was granted tax-exemption in the US. No real explanation of this turnaround by the IRS has ever been offered. It has been alleged that corruption was involved, but the IRS claim that with the death of its founder, Ron Hubbard, money was no longer pouring into anyone's personal bank accounts. Instead, it accrues to the control of David Miscavige, who continues to mistreat the followers[12] and accumulate a mountain of cash with no real objective for its use. Miscavige lives the lifestyle of the super-rich, surrounded by cowed believers who respond, without question, to his every demand.[13] How did this deplorable situation come about? To better understand, we have to wind back to the beginnings of the source of Scientology: Lafayette Ronald Hubbard.

ron Hubbard - the Source

Hubbard was born in Nebraska, in the US, in 1911. He grew up in Montana, in his maternal grandfather's household. He seems to have led a happy and protected childhood. He would later claim that his grandfather owned "a quarter of Montana", but this exaggeration is quite typical of Hubbard's fabulisms. In fact, Lafe Waterbury had a "half section" of 320 acres.[14] Hubbard said that as a child he was "breaking broncos",[15] though a school friend says that he was actually afraid of his grandfather's horses.

Hubbard claimed to have been a "blood brother" of the Blackfoot Indians, as an infant, though in his first novel, *Buckskin Brigades*, which is about this people, he said his source was someone who had lived with them, and made no mention of any personal connection. No American Indian people actually created blood brothers: it is a Hollywood myth. In the 1980s, Hubbard was finally inducted into the tribe by an eighth blood, who happened to be a Scientologist, to make up for this anomaly.[16]

Hubbard's father was absent in the Navy, through much of his childhood, but was able to take his wife, and their only child on two trips to the Orient. Hubbard would later claim to have studied with gurus in India, China and Tibet, but when his own contemporary journals of his two holidays in China became available, they showed that his only comment about the wisdom of the East concerned a visit to a lamasery, where he said that monks' voices sounded "like bullfrogs". He visited neither India nor Tibet.

Hubbard dropped out of college, but claimed to be a "nuclear physicist". His grades in atomic physics show that he failed the course. Nonetheless, he would repeatedly claim to be a "scientist", although there is no evidence of this beyond his boast.

L. Ron Hubbard Heads Movie Cruise Among Old American Piratical Haunts

Ray Heimburger, University Engineer, Also on Crew of Old Four-Mast Schooner Which Will Record on Celluloid Famous Pirate Strongholds

Contrary to popular belief, windjammer days are not over, and Romance refuses to die the death—at least for fifty young gentlemen rovers who will set sail on the schooner Doris Hamlin from Baltimore on June 20 for the pirate haunts of the Spanish Main.

Heading the cruise, which is called the Caribbean Motion Picture Expedition, is L. Ron Hubbard of the George Washington University Engineering School. Acting in the capacity of supercargo is Ray Heimburger, also a G. W. U. engineer.

These fifty men come from all over the country, a hand-picked crew of adventurers who, realizing the futility of finding jobs in this season of negative prosperity, are gambling their last dimes to film a series of pictures which are to concern the buccaneering days.

Their ship is the Doris Hamlin of Baltimore, a 1061 gross ton, fourmast, 200 feet by 38 feet sailing ship which they are equipping with labs and berths. Doris is one of the old school.

(Continued on Page 6, Col. 2)

Hubbard also spoke of leading expeditions, as a young man, but his own article, published after his "Caribbean Motion Picture Expedition" shows that he failed to achieve any of its objectives, as almost all of his student crew abandoned ship along the way.

Hubbard's "Alaskan Radio Experimental Expedition" found him stranded in Ketchikan, Alaska, where he charmed the locals with his radio

appearances, but made no significant contribution to anything but his own coffers. He made a meager living churning out "penny a word" pulp fiction.

With war on the horizon, Hubbard scrambled to find a safe place in the US Navy. He was posted to the PR department, because he had published a variety of adventure stories, so had some grasp of writing. When he joined the navy, Hubbard abandoned his first wife and their two young children, and paid nothing further to their upkeep.

In his later writings, Hubbard made many claims about his naval career, but in 1950, admitted to an interviewer that his "war wounds" consisted of "ulcers, conjunctivitis, deteriorating eyesight and something wrong with my feet."[17] He would boast that he had been the first US casualty of the war - wounded by machine gun fire - and had rowed himself from the wreck of the

USS Edsel to Australia. He never explained how a man with machine gun bullet wounds managed to row over 800 miles. His personal nurse later testified that there were no scars from bullet wounds on his body.[18]

Hubbard's own accounts are contradictory. He claimed to have been lamed with "physical injuries to hip and back" and "blinded with injured optic nerves" at the end of WWII, but this is contradicted by a lecture where he claimed to have won a fight against three petty officers, only two weeks before the war finished.[19]

THE CROWLEY CONNECTION

After the war, Hubbard practiced hypnosis, even performing on stage, and moved in with notorious "sex magician" Jack Parsons, a follower of Aleister Crowley, who believed himself to be the Beast 666. Together, Parsons and Hubbard performed homosexual rituals intended to incarnate the Scarlet Woman, spoken of in the biblical *Revelation of St John*. The Scarlet Woman is the precursor of the Anti-Christ. Court records show that Hubbard tricked Parsons out of his considerable savings, before putting to sea with Parsons' girlfriend. Hubbard married this woman, without divorcing his first wife.

In 1947, Hubbard wrote to the Veterans Administration pleading for psychiatric treatment to overcome bouts of depression. In this letter he said, "I cannot account for nor rise above long periods of moroseness and suicidal inclinations..."[20] Hubbard later told his followers that he had cured himself of war wounds at precisely this time. He claimed a pension for his ulcers until the day he died, despite these assurances. Hubbard continued to take powerful barbiturate drugs, first prescribed for his alleged ulcers, for at least two decades, and admitted in a recorded lecture that he had become addicted to them.[21]

Hubbard was also practicing self-hypnosis, using a mixture of hypnotic suggestion and magical incantation, in a set of "affirmations". He told himself, for instance, "Men are your slaves" and "elemental spirits are your slaves." And added: "Your psychology is advanced and true and wonderful. It hypnotizes people. It predicts their emotions, for you are their ruler."[22] In these affirmations, Hubbard makes much of his connection to his "holy Guardian", a spirit whom he believed watched over him. He later told an aide that his book *Dianetics: the Modern Science of Mental Health* was dictated by this spirit, whom he also called "the Empress."[23]

ADL NTA FILES

RE: LaFayette Ronald HUBBARD,
C-7017422
Lt, USNR 113392

F I L E D

OCT 2 9 1947

B. C. AA. 25

Box 297
North Hollywood, Calif.
October 15, 1947

Medical
VETERANS ADMINISTRATION
Los Angeles, 25, Calif.

Gentlemen;

This is a request for treatment.

My residence is north of North Hollywood,
but I attend school at Geller Theater Workshop,
Fairfax and Wilshire, Los Angeles. It would be
appreciated if any out-physician selected would
be located near my school as I have a vacant
hour and a half from 1 to 2:30 four days each
week at school. I work at night six days per week.

I was placed on certain medication back
east and have continued it at my own expense.

After trying and failing for two years
to regain my equilibrium in civil life, I am
utterly unable to approach anything like my
own competence. My last physician informed me
that it might be very helpful if I were to be
examined and perhaps treated psychiatrically
or even by a psycho-analyst. Toward the end
of my service I avoided out of pride any mental
examinations, hoping that time would balance
a mind which I had every reason to suppose was
seriously affected. I cannot account for nor
rise above long periods of moroseness and suicidal
inclinations, and have newly come to realize that
I must first triumph above this before I can hope
to rehabilitate myself at all.

I cannot leave school or what little work
I am doing for hospitalization due to many
obligations, but I feel I might be treated
outside, possibly with success. I cannot,
myself, afford such treatment.

Would you please help me?

Sincerely,

L. Ron Hubbard

16

DIANETICS

In the late 1940s, unable to meet his financial needs by writing pulp fiction, Hubbard wrote to his agent that he had found a new way to make money, and plenty of it.[24] This was the beginning of Dianetics. At first, Hubbard simply used deep trance hypnosis to address ailments. There was nothing new in this method, but Hubbard managed to convince a medical publisher to sign up a book. His closest colleague at that time, who wrote an appendix for that book, has said that Hubbard decided to abandon deep trance work and use light trance or "reverie", instead, because hypnosis was unpopular.[25]

Dianetics was based on work abandoned by Freud at the beginning of the century. Freud had commented that it had little therapeutic value, and made clients dependent upon the therapist.[26] During World War II, several psychiatrists had used Freud's abandoned method with traumatized military personnel, and found that under barbiturates, such as phenobarbital, there seemed to be some success.[27] These psychiatrists soon gave up the work, but Hubbard rode a wave of popular interest with the publication of *Dianetics: the Modern Science of Mental Health*, in May 1950. 150,000 copies of the book were sold, and Dianetics clubs began all over the US, and throughout the English-speaking world.

Hubbard claimed that his techniques - which supposedly took away the command value of incidents buried in the unconscious or "reactive" mind - could produce remarkable cures. He claimed to have cured asthma, poor eyesight and even cancer.[28] He would later claim that his techniques had successfully raised people from the dead.[29]

By emptying the trauma from the "reactive mind" a "clear" would be produced, who would be totally rational and have a genius IQ. However, Dr. Joseph Winter, who had worked with Hubbard during the months preceding the writing of this book, became suspicious of Hubbard's many claims of cure. Despite high sales, the publisher withdrew the book and replaced it with Winter's critique.[30] The presentation of a "Dianetic Clear" to an audience of 6,000 at the Shrine Auditorium, in Los Angeles, proved catastrophic, when despite her purported perfect memory, she was unable to even remember the color of Hubbard's neck tie, when he turned his back.

Los Angeles Examiner * Wed., April 11, 1951   Sec. I—9

'Dianetic' Hubbard Accused of Plot to Kidnap Wife

Hiding of Baby Charged to Dianetics Author

Wife Says Her Husband Conspired to Conceal 13-Month-Old Girl Missing Since Feb. 23

Wife Accuses Dianetics Hubbard of Kidnaping Her

DIANETICS INVENTOR SUED FOR DIVORCE

Wife's Complaint Charges He Subjected Her to 'Scientific Torture Experiments'

Ron Hubbard Insane, Says His Wife

IN COURT ACTION—Mrs. Sara Hubbard (above) has charged that dianetics founder mate, L. Ron Hubbard, and two other men kidnapped her and concealed her daughter, 13, from her.
Los Angeles Examiner photo

The enthusiasm for the fad of Dianetics fell away, and, in divorce papers, Hubbard's second wife alleged that he had tortured her - leading to deafness in one ear. Similar allegations were made by his first wife. By this time, Hubbard was living with another woman, in Los Angeles. He kidnapped his baby daughter with his second wife and took her to Cuba. After three months, his second wife, desperate for the return of her daughter, withdrew her allegations.

SCIENTOLOGY

The New Jersey Medical Authority filed a suit for practicing medicine without a license against Hubbard's Foundation, and he sold all rights in Dianetics to a Kansas oilman. Hubbard's assistant was caught stealing the mailing lists of the Kansas Foundation. Hubbard sent out over 30 pleading letters to that list. By February 1952, the bubble had burst, and, with the loss of Dianetics, Hubbard had to dream up a new subject. He turned to the writings of Aleister Crowley,[31] who reveled in the title "the wickedest man in the world". Crowley openly advocated drug abuse and promiscuous sex. He died, addicted to heroin, in 1947. In a lecture, Hubbard would falsely call Crowley, "My very good friend."[32] They did not actually meet, and, in correspondence, Crowley called Hubbard a confidence trickster.[33] Hubbard adopted Crowley's belief in reincarnation, and took his symbol of the crossed out cross for his new belief.[34]

Hubbard had earlier told friends that the best way to make a fortune was to start a religion,[35] and by 1953, he was asking his deputy her opinion on the "religion angle" and suggesting that it might revive his flagging financial situation.[36] In December, that year, he filed papers for three "churches", including the Church of Scientology, in Camden, New Jersey. He kept these registrations secret, and later claimed that the first church had been registered two months later by one of his followers, in California.

Hubbard continued to attract believers who edited sections from his lectures into new books. After *Dianetics*, he would not actually write another book. Among these compilations is *Scientology: A History of Man*, which Hubbard claimed to be "a cold blooded and factual account of your last sixty trillion years." He would later extend his dating of the universe to "quadrillions", but here he put forward his view that human beings are descended from clams. This has led opponents to call believers "clams", in ridicule.

Hubbard was joined by his oldest son, L. Ron Hubbard Jr. usually called Nibs, for the production of *History of Man*. Nibs claimed that his father gave him amphetamine drugs and simply asked him to recite his hallucinations. These became the "cold blooded and factual account." Nibs worked at the top of Scientology for seven years, eventually arguing with his father and leaving, in 1959. He claimed that his father never ceased to practice "sex magick", and was a multiple drug abuser. Other sources support this last claim, and Hubbard actually recommended the use of amphetamines in his early work.[37] He was an inveterate smoker, with a 120-a-day cigarette habit.[38] During his waking hours, he almost always had a lit cigarette to hand. Over the years, many people also saw him drink excessive amounts of alcohol.

One former secretary said that Hubbard would ask her about a topic over breakfast, and then give an account of her response in his afternoon lecture. Research into Hubbard's ideas shows that most were clearly plagiarized.[39] He even tempted his followers by referring to the origin of ideas in his lectures, but few ever take the time to check.

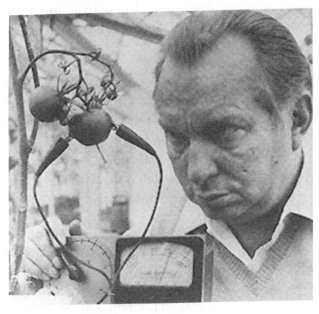

Hubbard's following was largely in the English-speaking world. He travelled between the USA, England and South Africa, with occasional forays into the antipodes. In 1959, he moved his headquarters to East Grinstead, in England. There he gave an interview to the press about his experiments on tomatoes. Ignorant of the perennial nature of tomatoes, he claimed to have created an "ever-bearing" variety.

After the demise of Dianetics, Scientology limped along, with perhaps a few thousand followers. Then, in 1963, the Australian state of Victoria announced an Inquiry into Hubbard's brainchild, which generated media interest and Inquiries elsewhere. Suddenly, thousands of people became interested in Scientology, which caught the popular anti-establishment wave.

THE SEA ORGANIZATION

Hubbard had fled to Rhodesia, after being caught trying to pass a prescription for barbiturate drugs in a pharmacy in England. He was expelled from Rhodesia, after his assistant was caught breaking into government offices.[40] Hubbard was declared an undesirable alien by the British government, and took to the high seas with a small crew, who became known as the Sea Organization.

For six years, the Sea Organization plied the waters of the Mediterranean, being thrown out of one port after another. Hubbard surrounded himself with the teenage daughters of his followers, who wore white "hot pants." They were trained to bark his orders at members of the crew in imitation of his own angry style.

Students are thrown overboard
for gross out tech and bequeathed
to the deep!

During this time, Hubbard introduced "overboarding" where errant Scientologists would be hurled from the deck of one of his vessels into the sea. Subjects of this practice have described its terrifying effects. Indeed, from publicizing a method of reducing trauma, Hubbard was now deliberately inducing it. Hubbard published his own photographs of this demeaning violation of human rights.[41]

While at sea, Hubbard also punished dissenting followers by confining them in the dark, fetid atmosphere of the chain lockers - where the anchor chains were kept while at sea. Children as young as four spent days in the dark, wet, rat-infested chain lockers, under Hubbard's orders.

Eventually, the Sea Organization was forced ashore, when no Mediterranean port would allow the Scientologists access. They landed in Florida, where, under the guise of the United Churches of Florida, they bought up properties in Clearwater and established the Flag Land Base. Hubbard was driven into hiding because of numerous legal suits. This did not stop him from personally orchestrating a harassment campaign against the mayor of Clearwater, Gabe Cazares.

RACKET EXPOSED

PETER GOODWIN
JIM STATHIS
POLLY STATHIS
PETER KNIGHT
MRS. KNIGHT
NORA GOODWIN
RON FROST
MARGARET FROST
NINA COLLINGWOOD
FREDA GAIMAN
FRANK MANLEY
MARY ANN TAYLOR
GEORGE WATERIDGE

are hereby declared Suppressive Persons for pretending to have and distribute forged and altered "Upper Level Materials" which were of a Research nature and not for distribution.

All Certificates and Awards are cancelled.

1. Having stolen or illegally procured these dangerous materials (at the instigation of a Psychiatrist) these persons did plot to misuse them to cause Insanity and Death.

2. False report for money that they would furnish the real materials.

3. They are declared Enemies of mankind, the planet and all life.

4. They are fair game.

5. No amnesty may ever cover them.

6. If they ever come to a Qual Division they are to be run on reverse processes.

7. Any Sea Organization member contacting any of them is to use Auditing Process R2-45.

8. The Criminals Prosecution Bureau is to find any and all crimes in their pasts and have them brought to court and prison.

The Public Distribution of False or Forbidden or Dangerous Data is a Suppressive Act and a High Crime.

Founder

SAINT HILL FIELD STAFF MEMBER AWARDS (continued)

HEALING PO IN THE FIE

(HCO Policy Letter of 7 Apr

BY L. RON HUBE

"The HCO Policy Letter 27, 1964, is now binding auditors and field staff memb

Many field auditors do that they damage their own tion and usefulness by be volved with the very ill and

The only thing a field audi really, without going down, mote, run meetings and do s as field staff members of th org. But whether they are Field Auditors including F and HQS must abide caref policy and inform those p seek to persuade them tc insane or very ill that "it mittee of Evidence offens HCO policy" and thus get free. I have seen too many fi fail by their becoming enta psychos and chronically sic fail to protect them fro mistake.

Excerpt from HCO Pol October 27, 1964:

HEALING

Any process labelled "he or new, refers to healing by

In 1977, in the largest raid in its history, the FBI took immense amounts of documents from Scientology's Los Angeles and Washington DC offices. Eleven years earlier, in 1966, in response to government inquiries, Hubbard had created the Guardian's Office, with his third wife, Mary Sue, as its nominal head. Branch One of the Guardian's Office dealt with "covert" operations.

In 1965, Hubbard had introduced the "fair game law", whereby opponents could be lied to, tricked, sued and even "destroyed" by Scientologists. When the Australian Inquiry in Victoria proved thoroughly negative and the state government decided to ban Scientology, Hubbard urged his followers to murder the head of that inquiry. He issued similar orders against defecting Scientologists.[42]

Oct 30 - Anybody - L
If anyone does
anything to get
any of these
organizations in
bad publicity,
such as narcotics
charges, drunk
driving or other
unsavory data,
I have a policy -

I will beat
their teeth in
personally.

Sincerely -
L

Hubbard often expressed his paranoid loathing for critics. Towards the end of his life, in 1982, before he descended in dementia, he wrote: "Time and again since 1950, the vested interests which pretend to run the world (for their own appetites and profit) have mounted full-scale attacks. With a running dog press and slavish government agencies the forces of evil have launched their lies and sought, by whatever twisted means, to check and destroy Scientology. What is being decided in this arena is whether mankind has a chance to go free or be smashed and tortured as an abject subject of the power elite."

Hubbard's attitude towards criticism was far from compassionate: "if anyone is getting industrious trying to enturbulate [upset] or stop Scientology or its activities, I can make Captain Bligh look like a Sunday school teacher. There is probably no limit on what I would do to safeguard man's only road to freedom against persons who, disdaining [Scientology] processing, seek to stop Scientology or hurt Scientologists."[43]

As early as 1955, Hubbard expressed his policy towards anyone who used his techniques without approval: "The law can be used very easily to harass, and enough harassment on somebody … will generally be sufficient to cause his professional decease. If possible, of course, ruin him utterly."[44] Over the next decades, following this dictum, Scientology became the most litigious organization in history, filing tens of thousands of suits to silence its opponents. Thankfully, with the drive for public acceptance as a religion, this practice has slowed down considerably in the last decade.

SECRET

(A)

DDG US

DG INFO US

12 March 76

RE: PREDICTION IN CW
Yours of 10 March 76

L.

Dear Duke,

You asked for a chart of enemy lines used up to this point for CW attack after research of the files was done.

Attached is this chart. It looks complete to me.

From this I see the areas of priority to infiltrate are:

1. SPT
2. Mayor
3. Channel 13 TV
4. Snyder
5. Florida Attorney General
6. Florida State Attorney (Russell)

As things have been quite hectic with me the last two days I wanted to send this to you to go over. Any changes or additions you want to make would be fine.

Love,

Dick

DW/mw

In 1967, Hubbard approved Guardian's Office investigations of the British Prime Minister and a hostile press baron by "professional intelligence agents."[45] Members of Parliament in several European countries had agents planted next to them.[46] Critics were to be silenced by whatever means necessary. Under Project Snow White, Scientologists were tasked to infiltrate 136 government agencies with a total of 5000 agents.[47] Hundreds of thousands of documents were stolen, leading to prosecutions in Canada and the US.

Eleven officials of the Guardian's Office were sentenced to prison terms in the US, for their part in the burglaries and theft of documents, as well as kidnapping and false imprisonment.

The Sentencing Memorandum for two of the GO executives read: "a review of the documents seized in the two Los Angeles ... searches ... show the incredible and sweeping nature of the criminal conduct of the defendants and or the organization which they led. These crimes include the infiltration and theft of documents from a number of prominent private national and world organizations, law firms and newspapers; the execution of smear campaigns and baseless law suits to destroy private individuals who had attempted to exercise their First Amendment rights to freedom of expression; the framing of private citizens who had been critical of Scientology, including the forging of documents which led to the indictment of at least one innocent person; violation of the civil rights of prominent private figures and public officials. These are but a few of the criminal acts not covered in the "uncontested" stipulation of evidence ... The evidence in this case and the documents seized by the FBI in Los Angeles establish beyond peradventure that the Church and its leadership had, over the years, approved, condoned and engaged in gross and widespread illegality. One, indeed, wonders how it can even be suggested that the defendants and their organization did not make illegal activities part and parcel of their daily work.[48]

Hubbard would remain in hiding for the last decade of his life, by which time there were more than 300 legal writs against him. He was named as a co-conspirator in the Guardian's Office case.

RELIGION

Sooner or later Excalibur will be published and I may have a chance to get some name recognition out of it so as to pave the way to articles and comments which are my ideas of writing heaven.

Living is a pretty grim joke, but a joke just the same. The entire function of man is to survive. Not "for what" but just to survive. The outermost limit of endeavor is creative work. Anything less is too close to simple survival until death happens along. So I am engaged in striving to maintain equilibrium sufficient to at last realize survival in a way to astound the gods. I turned the thing up so its up to me to survive in a big way. Personal immortality is only to be gained through the printed word, barred note or painted canvas or hard granite. Foolishly perhaps, but determined none the less, I have high hopes of smashing my name into history so violently that it will take a legendary form even if all the books are destroyed. That goal is the real goal as far as I am concerned. Things which stand too consistently in its way make me nervous. It's a pretty big job. In a hundred years Roosevelt will have been forgotten - which gives some idea of the magnitude of my attempt. And all this boils and froths inside my head and I'm miserable when I am blocked. Let the next man concentrate upon "peace" and "contentment". When life was struck into me something else accompanied it. And when I leave things in the lap of the gods who seem to be interested in my destiny, boy, things happen!

My fight right now is to get into a spot where I can tide across the gap until the next blaze. Excalibur may be fought, accepted or forgotten. I don't care. I seem to be the only one that has attained actual personal contact with it. Others take it mentally and seem to be at a loss to apply it. When I wrote it I gave myself an education which outranks that of anyone else. I don't know but it might seem that it takes terrific brain work to get the thing assembled and useable in the head. I do know that I could formulate a political platform, for instance, which would encompass the support of the unemployed, the industrialist and the clerk and day laborer all at one and the same time. And enthusiastic support it would be. Things are due for a bust in the next half a dozen years. Wait and see.

Writing action pulp doesn't have much agreement with what I want to do because it retards my progress by demanding incessant attention and, further, actually weakens my name. So you see I've got to do something about it and at the same time strengthen the old financial position.

Anyway, I won't burden you with any more of that sort of thing. But the things I do often seem pretty weird when judged from the standpoint of nice, quiet surroundings and peaceful old age. I haven't started to get old and I won't seek peace until I'm stretched on a marble slab. And I won't be stretched on any marble

In the 1960s, Hubbard gathered together his elaborate series of hypnotic procedures into the "Bridge". Scientologists move through almost thirty levels. Beyond "Clear" Hubbard introduced the upper levels, which are supposed to lead to fantastic supernatural powers, though since their release in the 1960s, no Scientologist has ever made the slightest demonstration of such powers.

Hubbard sold the idea of immortality to his followers: "For thousands of years men have sought the state of complete spiritual freedom from the endless cycle of birth and death and have sought personal immortality containing full awareness, memory and ability as a spirit independent of the flesh ... In Scientology this state has been attained. It has been achieved not on a temporary basis, subject to relapse, but on a stable plane of full awareness and ability, unqualified by accident or deterioration. And not limited to a few. We call this state "Operating Thetan"."[49]

However, in a letter to his first wife, written in 1938 (and subsequently copyrighted by one of his organizations), Hubbard admitted that he had no belief in spiritual immortality: "Personal immortality is only to be gained through the printed word, barred note or painted canvas or hard granite. Foolishly perhaps, but determined none the less, I have high hopes of smashing my name into history so violently that it will take a legendary form even if all the books are destroyed. That goal is the real goal as far as I am concerned. Things which stand too consistently in its way make me nervous ... It's a big joke, this living. God was feeling sardonic the day He created the Universe. So it's rather up to at least one man every few centuries to pop up and come just as close to making Him swallow his laughter as possible."[50]

In the late 1940s, Hubbard told several people that the best way to make a fortune is to start a religion. He finally achieved his ambition in 1953, but, in a lecture given the year before, he said, "It must pay people to control people. Now, if you don't think that religion is a control basis and doesn't operate just in one direction, you should look at some of the implants on the track." "Implants" are incidents of deliberate hypnosis and the "track" is simply the past. Hubbard is saying that religion exists to control people.[51]

As early as 1952, Hubbard claimed that through Scientology training, anyone would be "capable of dismissing illness and aberration from others at will." Hubbard renamed the soul the "thetan" - a lisped version of "satan" - and called his grades above Clear the Operating Thetan levels. In 1967, Hubbard introduced Operating Thetan Section III. The material remained secret, until former member Robert Kaufman made it public in his book

Inside Scientology, in 1972. Scientologists have publicly denied the contents of OT III, even though Hubbard's hand-written instructions and his taped lectures have long since been publicly available.

Scientology has little to offer beyond OT III. OT levels IV, V, VI and VII are all concerned with the "body thetans" or stuck spirits found on OT III. There is only one level beyond this - although Hubbard claimed to have prepared 15, nothing was found after his death. To take OT VIII, Scientologists undergo rigorous "security checking" on a lie detector, to ensure that they have no "evil purposes". The level is only available on the Scientology cruise ship, the Freewinds, and students are monitored on camera from the moment they pick up the material, to make sure that they make no copies and take no notes. Defectors have said that this level calls Jesus a pedophile and asserts that Hubbard himself is God.

CLAIMS

News in Brief

WEDNESDAY, FEBRUARY 15, 1978

Compiled from the Los Angeles Times the Los
Angeles Times-Washington Post News Service and
major wire and supplementary news agencies.

The American founder of the Church of Scientology. L. Ron Hubbard, was sentenced in absentia by a French court to four years in prison and fined $7,000 after he and two of his French assistants were convicted of defrauding new members with promises of health and wealth. The two assistants, both of whom have left France, received lesser sentences. Hubbard is thought to be living on a yacht off Bermuda and could not be reached for comment.

Los Angeles Times, 15 February 1978

Hubbard made many claims for his practices, none of which have been independently verified, despite his frequent boast that he was a "scientist". For instance, Hubbard said, "This is useful knowledge. With it the blind again see, the lame walk, the ill recover, the insane become sane and the sane become saner." In the same 1952 text, he claimed "Cancer has been eradicated."[52] Sadly, many Scientologists have died of cancer, perhaps because they did not seek medical help rapidly enough, because of Hubbard's disdain for medical treatment.

Of his state of Clear - first promised unreservedly in 1950 - Hubbard declared that "A Clear has over 135 I.Q., a vibrant personality, glowing health, good memory, amazing vitality, self-control, happiness and more. The most valuable thing you will do for yourself, and for your family, friends and Mankind is attain the state of Clear. You can achieve Clear - not in years but within months through the most advanced technology of the human spirit - Scientology."[53]

> 'Plaintiffs [the Church of Scientology] have abused the federal court system by using it, inter alia, to destroy their opponents rather than to try to resolve an actual dispute ... This constitutes extraordinary, malicious, wanton, and oppressive conduct.'
>
> —U.S. Special Master James Kolts

Scientologists are instructed to be fanatical, as Hubbard put it: "When somebody enrolls, consider he or she has joined up for the duration of the universe - never permit an "open-minded" approach. If they're going to quit let them quit fast. If they enrolled, they're aboard; and if they're aboard, they're here on the same terms as the rest of us - win or die in the attempt. Never let them be half-minded about being Scientologists ... We'd rather have you dead than incapable."[54]

CHRISTIANITY

Privately, Hubbard agreed with Aleister Crowley's criticisms of Christianity. In one article that only remained in print briefly, he said that once the universe was "cleared" by Scientology, God would be found hiding under a rock.[55] Hubbard also said that Jesus was a fabrication and a part of the "implanting" of the supposed OT III incident: "There was no Christ."[56] Hubbard also said, "God is a problem itself germane to this universe. If you go into other universes and ask who is god around here, the people wouldn't quite know what you were talking about. God just happens to be the trick of this universe."[57] Further, Hubbard said that religion is, "basically a control mechanism ... You will find the cross as a symbol all over the universe, and the Christ legend as [a hypnotic] implant ... a million years ago."[58]

When he secretly registered his first Church of Scientology, in December 1953, Hubbard also registered the Church of American Science, which was to recruit Christians and lead them to something "better" - meaning Scientology: "The Church of American Science is a Christian religion. It believes in the Holy Bible, Jesus is the Savior of man ... People who belong to that church are expected to be Christians ... We take somebody in as a Church of American Science [member]. It doesn't disagree with his baptism ... and he could gradually slide over into some sort of better, wider activity such as the Church of Scientology ... we have provided stepping stones to Scientology."[59]

Christianity

Hubbard claimed to have scientifically researched other religions: "With rapidity and a Meter [a lie detector] it can be shown that Heaven is a false dream and that the old religion was based on a very painful lie, a cynical betrayal. What does this do to any religious nature of Scientology? It strengthens it. New religions always overthrow the false gods of the old, they do something to better man. We can improve man. We can show the old gods are false. But I imagine when we finally manage to communicate with beetles under rocks and free them, we'll no doubt find the Creator of Heaven who 43+ Trillion years ago designed and built the Pearly Gates and entrapped us all ... This ... Bulletin ... is scientific research and is not in any way based upon the mere opinion of the researcher."[60]

Hubbard was determined to create the perception that his hypnotic techniques were religious in nature. In a letter to his business manager, in April 1953, Hubbard wrote: "We don't want a clinic. We want one in operation but not in name. Perhaps we could call it a Spiritual Guidance Center ... we could put in nice desks and our boys in neat blue with diplomas on the walls and 1. Knock psychotherapy into history and 2. Make enough money to shine up my operating scope and 3. Keep the HAS [Hubbard Association of Scientologists] solvent. It is a problem in practical business. I await your reaction on the religion angle."[61]

HYPNOSIS

THE AUTHOR

L. Ron Hubbard's stories of the sea, adventure, fantasy and science fiction have appeared under six pen names in over seventy-two national publications. Famous for his work which has been p r i n t e d in AS-TOUNDING SCIENCE FICTION, Mr. Hubbard's writing has b e e n featured in s u c h periodicals as UNKNOWN, FANTASY B O O K, STARTLING STORIES & THRILL-ING WONDER STORIES. Some of his best known novels are FEAR, THE END IS NOT YET, and the DOC METHUSELAH series. Mr. Hubbard has had five books publish-ed. These include BUCKSKIN BRI-GADE, FINAL BLACKOUT (Had-ley), DEATH'S DEPUTY (Fantasy

L. Ron Hubbard

Publishing Co.), SLAVES OF SLEEP (Shasta), and this volume, TRITON. Also to be published soon by Fantasy Publishing Company is his novel KINGSLAYER. This story has never before appeared in print.

Mr Hubbard is a member of The Explorer's Club of New York y, Theta Tau Fraternity, and the Author's League of America. During the second World War he served in the Navy as Command-ing Officer of Escort vessels in the North Atlantic, and later in the Pacific zone. His leisure hours are devoted to the study and practice of hynotism, photography, fishing and traveling and he is an auth-ority on ancient and medieval navigation.

From his teens, Hubbard was an eager student of hypnosis. The author's biography for his novel *Triton*, says that "his leisure hours are devoted to the study and practice of hypnotism." He was well known for hypnotizing people at fan club gatherings, in the late 1940s. Indeed, the original method used for his Dianetics was deep trance hypnosis, but when his book was commissioned, Hubbard told an associate that as deep trance was unpopular, he would instead use the "reverie" or light trance method.[62] Hubbard admitted that the "reverie" technique was hypnotic and cancelled it, in 1951. It was reintroduced, without comment, in the late 1970s and forms part of the "Book One Course" which is used to introduce new recruits to Scientology.[63]

The term "hypnosis" has aroused much controversy. Probably the most exacting definition was given by Dr. Milton Erickson, who said that hypnosis is an interaction between people, which accesses altered states of consciousness.

Steven Hassan, a leading expert on hypnosis and cults, has called the Training Routines used in Scientology, "the most overt use of hypnosis by any cult."[64] Scientologists remain ignorant of the fundamental techniques of hypnosis - repetition, fixation and mimicry - and believe that the euphoric states they achieve in "auditing" are beneficial, rather than transitory altered states.

Contemporary psychology has demonstrated that most mental processes occur below consciousness. A hypnotherapist accesses the unconscious mind in an attempt to place beneficial suggestions there, which will have the same motivating force upon the individual as his or her own decisions. In hypnotherapy, the client gives permission for this process to happen. In Scientology, the process happens without consent. Indeed, Scientologists are assured that the procedures of "auditing" are not hypnotic and actually undo hypnosis.

Hubbard asserted that everything that exists is a product of consciousness: "reality is an agreement", according to Hubbard, and the universe is "an agreed upon apparency." From this perspective, Scientology seeks to change the individual's perception of reality, and replace it with Hubbard's notions, at the same time pretending that the individual is becoming more aware. Although Scientologists progressively abandon their own thinking, instead adopting Hubbard's, they believe that they are becoming more "self-determined."

Scientology claims to be scientific, but factually, it is impossible to undertake Scientology "auditing" without submitting to beliefs that have not been scientifically validated, such as reincarnation, possession by spirits (or "body thetans") and the influence of trauma. Hubbard records only one attempt at scientific verification, where a volunteer was subjected to "pain-drug hypnosis" and a subsequent attempt to recall the words spoken during this episode. As Hubbard says, the experiment failed.[65]

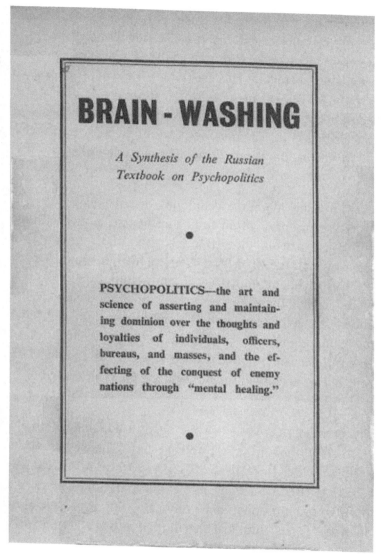

Restrictions are placed upon Scientologists to prevent them from reaching a critical understanding of Scientology. Explanation of Hubbard's work is forbidden ("verbal tech"); the materials must be quoted exactly, so discussion is highly restricted. Dissent from the materials is also forbidden. The Scientologist's realizations in "auditing" must align with Hubbard's pronouncements on the nature of reality. Any disagreement with Hubbard, or his teachings, will lead to an interview with the "Ethics Officer", an official of Scientology's internal police.

The Scientologist must not talk about his "case" or problems, other than to his "auditor, which inhibits close relationships. The "technology" of Scientology is always right (even when Hubbard changed it, every few months). Failure to achieve spectacular success (which is to say, euphoric states) is attributed to the "preclear", never to the "technology". Scientologists are led to believe that criticism of Scientology or Hubbard always stems from the critic's guilt. The member's attention is focused inward and deflected from consideration of Hubbard's or Scientology's faults.

Through the use of intensely hypnotic techniques, disguised as counseling, the believer's entire perception and belief system is over-ridden by Scientology. Scientologists are not allowed to talk about the demon possession sold as therapy on the "upper levels", so are further separated from normal communication. Scientologists accept only Hubbard's perception of reality. He derided hypnotherapy, psychology, analysis, meditation and religious counseling, claiming that no other system is effective. Although he printed long lists of acknowledgements to earlier thinkers, including Freud, Jesus and the Buddha,[66] Hubbard said that his own work was the only breakthrough in the fields of the mind and spirit in "50,000 years."

Hubbard was fully aware of the subtle use of language. In a policy letter, called *Propaganda by Redefinition of Words*, Hubbard said: "The trick is - WORDS ARE REDEFINED TO MEAN SOMETHING ELSE TO THE ADVANTAGE OF THE PROPAGANDIST."[67] This is alarming, as Hubbard left not one but two dictionaries of his own redefinitions, each numbering 500 pages. No one has ever redefined so many words. Hubbard also dipped into marketing and public relations textbooks and was an avid user of such techniques, allied with his own hard-selling approach.[68]

the Suppressive Person Doctrine

As early as 1953, Hubbard started to call any critic a "merchant of fear."[69] In the 1960s, this term evolved into "Suppressive Person." According to an official Scientology website "A suppressive person is a person who seeks to suppress any betterment activity or group. The suppressive person, also called an antisocial personality, works to upset, continuously undermine, spread bad news and denigrate other people and their activities."[70] Anti-social personality is, of course, an alternative term for "sociopath" or "psychopath", borrowed from psychiatric literature.

According to Hubbard, Suppressive People speak in generalities ("everybody knows"); deal mainly in bad news; worsen communication they are relaying; fail to respond to psychotherapy (that is, Scientology); are surrounded by "cowed or ill associates or friends"; habitually select the wrong target or source; are unable to finish anything; willingly confess to alarming crimes, without any sense of responsibility for them; support only destructive groups; approve only destructive actions; detest help being given to others, and use "helping" as a pretext to destroy others; and they believe that no-one really owns anything. Over a thousand people have been declared "Suppressive" by the cult and members are forbidden any communication with us.

When his son, L. Ron Hubbard Jr. defected in 1959, Hubbard introduced "security checking". From that time, members have to answer long lists of questions - many of them highly personal - while attached to the electrodes of an "e-meter", which, as we have seen, Hubbard himself described as a form of lie detector. The answers are written down and lodged in the Scientologist's "ethics folder." There is ample evidence of such confessions - as they are now known - being used against defectors.[71]

When "security checking" proved ineffective in stemming the flow of defectors. Hubbard introduced the "fair game law", whereby anyone declared Suppressive is deprived of any human rights. Scientology has attacked its critics vigorously under the fair game law.

Another invidious practice is that of "disconnection", where Scientologists are ordered to cease any communication with designated "Suppressives." The cult frequently denies this practice, but the testimony of hundreds of former members and internal documents show that it is a core belief of Scientology.[72] Through the Suppressive Person doctrine, Fair Game and Disconnection, Scientology is able to insulate members from criticism and accurate information.

Scientologists are compelled to write "knowledge reports" denouncing any criticism of Hubbard or Scientology.[73] These reports are kept in dossiers by the "Ethics Office". A similar practice was used by the Nazi Gestapo.[74]

Infiltration

INTELLIGENCE SPECIALIST TRAINING ROUTINE - TR L

Purpose: To train the student to give a false statement with good TR-1. To train the student to outflow false data effectively.

Position: Same as TR-1.

Commands: Part 1 "Tell me a lie". Command given by coach. Part 2 interview type 2 WC by coach.

Training Stress: In Part 1 coach gives command, student originates a falsehood. Coach flunks for out TR 1 or TR 0. In Part 2 coach asks questions of the student on his background or a subject. Student gives untrue data of a plausible sort that the student backs up with further explanatory data upon the coach further questions. The coach flunks for out TR 0 and TR 1, and for student fumbling on question answers. The student should be coached on a gradient until he/she can lie facily.

Short example:

Coach: Where do you come from?

Student: I come from the Housewives Committee on Drug Abuse.

Coach: But you said earlier that you were single.

Student: Well, actually I was married but am divorced. I have 2 kids in the suburbs where I am a housewife, in fact I'm a member of the P.T.A.

Coach: What town is it that you live in?

Student: West Brighton

Coach: But there is no public school in West Brighton.

Student: I know. I send my children to school in Brighton, and that's where I'm a P.T.A. member.

Coach: Oh, and who is the Chairman there?

etc.

In Germany, Scientologists are forbidden work in the public service, because their first loyalty is to the cult. During the case against the eleven Guardian's Office members, in the US, it came out that a police officer who was a Scientologist had been using police computers to prevent the apprehension of a former Scientologist who was being held captive by the cult. Hubbard told his followers that they should infiltrate society: "Don't bother to get elected. Get a job on the secretarial staff or the bodyguard ... don't seek the co-operation of groups. Don't ask for permission. Just enter them and start functioning"[75]

Scientologists who work in the intelligence or "investigation" department are privy to an 800 page pack, which details methods of harassment and deception. The few Scientologists who have taken this course have to read several books about intelligence agencies and learn their techniques. The Office of Special Affairs Investigation Bureau has replaced the notorious Guardian's Office Branch One. The only change to the instructional materials is in the title. Otherwise, all 800 pages of this scurrilous course remain the same.

Hubbard summed up his philosophy with these words: "If attacked on some vulnerable point by anyone or anything or any organization, always find or manufacture enough threat against them to cause them to sue for peace ... Don't ever defend. Always attack ... The goal of the Department [of Government Affairs] is to bring the government and hostile philosophies or societies into a state of complete compliance with the goals of Scientology. This is done by high-level ability to control and in its absence by low-level ability to overwhelm. Introvert such agencies. Control such agencies ... Increasing amounts of order must be maintained by us at a governmental level against the possibility of finding our areas without governments."[76]

Scientology has developed many other groups, which have fed members into the parent organization. In 1966, Hubbard wrote, cynically, "Remember, CHURCHES ARE LOOKED UPON AS REFORM GROUPS. Therefore we must act like a reform group." [Emphasis in the original]

Narconon, a supposed drug rehabilitation group, was led by Hubbard aide, Colonel Mark Jones, under the direction of the Guardian's Office, but has always claimed to have been the brainchild of a heroin addict, who in fact returned to his addiction after taking the Narconon course. Narconon faces many legal suits in the US.

The Citizens Commission on Human Rights wages war on mental health professionals. Guardian's Office defectors have admitted to putting LSD into the toothpaste of psychiatrists at conventions, among other dirty tricks. Psychology professor Margaret Singer found dead rats nailed to the wooden steps of her home in California. CCHR luminary Jan Eastgate was charged for obstruction of justice, in Australia, for persuading an 11-year-old girl to withdraw her truthful allegations of sexual abuse by a Scientologist. The Scientologist was convicted on his own admission, years after the abuse. Charges against Eastgate were dropped, although there were seven witnesses to her actions.

Among the many groups associated with Scientology are the World Institute of Scientology Enterprises, the Association for Better Living and Education, Criminon, the Concerned Businessmen's Association and Applied Scholastics.

LITIGATION

Scientology has featured in thousands of court cases. Because of its policy that the "law can used very easily to harass" it has brought more suits than any organization in history. At one point, more than 3000 suits were withdrawn. Former member, Lawrence Wollersheim, fought for many years to eventually receive a payment of nine million dollars for the cult's induction of manic depression in him and the destruction of his family and his business.

In Canada, Judge Casey Hill won a libel action against the cult, which had defamed him in the attempt to hinder prosecution. The judgment in this case says, "Scientology was engaged in an unceasing and apparently unstoppable campaign to destroy Casey Hill and his reputation ... Scientology has not been deterred from its course of conduct by a previous judicial determination that its allegations were unfounded nor by its own knowledge that its principal allegation ... was false ... every aspect of this case demonstrates the very real and persistent malice of Scientology. Their actions preceding the publication of the libel, the circumstances of its publication and their subsequent actions in relation to both the search warrant proceedings and this action amply confirm and emphasize the insidious malice of Scientology."[77]

Recently, the cult has lost a fraud suit in France, leading to restrictions on Scientology practices, particularly the Purification Rundown, a regimen of multivitamins and sauna sweating, for hours each day. High doses of B vitamins can lead to hallucinations, which Scientologists are led to believe are the consequence of drugs lodged in their systems.

Scientology leader, David Miscavige, wants to achieve religious status throughout the world. To this end, the harassment has diminished significantly. With the internet and affordable cameras, harassment is easily reported. Nonetheless, in 2001, Miscavige said, "Shooting down enemies of Scientology has been like shooting ducks in a pond."[78]

Hubbard died in 1986, leaving $648 million, all of it taken from Scientology. By this time, he had his own 24-track recording studio, a 2000-piece camera collection, a race track, a lake with black swans and a herd of Aberdeen Angus bulls. To accumulate this fortune, Hubbard had ruined many of his followers and even withdrawn such necessities as toilet paper from his Sea Organization.

SEA ORGANIZATION

CONTRACT OF EMPLOYMENT

I,_____, DO HEREBY
AGREE to enter into employment with the SEA
ORGANIZATION and, being of sound mind, do
fully realize and agree to abide by its purpose
which is to get <u>ETHICS IN</u> on this <u>PLANET AND
THE UNIVERSE</u> and, fully and without reservation,
subscribe to the discipline, mores and conditions
of this group and pledge to abide by them.

THEREFORE, I CONTRACT MYSELF TO THE

SEA ORGANIZATION FOR THE NEXT BILLION

YEARS.

(As per Flag Order 232)

Date_____ Signed_____

In 1967, after he was thrown out of England, Hubbard collected a group of devoted believers, who came to be called the Sea Organization. Members dress in pseudo-naval uniforms and sign a *billion year* contract. Hubbard claimed that they were modeled on the Loyal Officers of the Galactic Confederation, who had followed Xenu's orders, 75 million years before.[79]

Sea Org members swear to follow "command intention", without question. They typically work a 90-hour week for a pittance. Since Hubbard's death, they are forbidden children and many members have been coerced into abortions, in keeping with this rule.

Fearing extradition to France on fraud charges, Hubbard fled to New York in late 1972. He returned to his ship, the Apollo, in Portugal, in September 1973. In or about November, he had a motorcycle accident on Tenerife. He published his orders starting the "rehabilitation project force," on January 4, 1974. It is most likely that he came up with the Rehabilitation Project Force while chair-bound, howling in pain as recovered from his accident. It is very likely based upon a reading of psychiatrist Robert Jay Lifton's *Thought Reform in Modern China*, which gives detailed descriptions of the Chinese "re-education" camps. The intention of this thought reform, both in the Chinese state and in Scientology is to bring about unwavering compliance.

If a Sea Org member fails to achieve high enough production statistics, or refuses orders, they will be assigned to the Rehabilitation Project Force or "RPF". The RPF typically lasts for several years, and some members may have been kept in this thought reform environment for decades. RPF members have often been denied contact with their children, for months or even years on end.

RPFers are reduced to the status of Untouchables, disdained by all other staff members. They are not allowed books or music, nor luxuries of any kind. They can only speak when spoken to and undertake hard manual labor, seven days a week, with no days off, including Christmas. They must eat the scraps from the already poorly fed crew and they live in stinking dormitories, sometimes without mattresses. If they are completely compliant, they are allowed to see their families every second week on a Friday evening. The slightest dissent will lose them even that basic human right.

RPFers are interrogated with exhausting "confessionals", some listing hundreds of questions. Careful note is taken of the most shameful events in the individual's life, which are noted in the "ethics folder". These interrogations take place using an E-meter, which is used as a lie detector.[80] At worst, as Hubbard says, "When the subject placed on the meter will not talk but can be made to hold cans (or can be held while the cans are strapped to the soles or placed under the armpit...) it is still possible to obtain full information from the subject."[81]

Perhaps the worst RPF is in Los Angeles, where tens of black-clad detainees rush silent and cowed between their tasks. They are usually to be found in the basement and the tunnels beneath the former Cedars of Lebanon Hospital, which has long been Scientology's headquarters in LA. The tunnels are a network of dimly lit corridors, lined with service pipes, which connect a warren of basement rooms. Among these rooms is the notorious Rats" Alley.

Rats Alley is an enormous, unlit, windowless room, with a ceiling less than four feet high. It is below the kitchens and the heat is sweltering. The room is full of huge rats and a host of giant cockroaches. RPFers are pushed into this airless space on wooden trolleys, and often spend whole days, from early morning until late at night, scraping at rancid oil and rotting waste. They make their way with a torch, amid swarms of cockroaches and huge scurrying rats.

Perhaps even worse than Rats Alley is the Morgue. RPFers have been forced to clean out the crematorium ovens, crawling among ashes and cleaning out abandoned human remains. There are also accounts of pregnant women who were forced to shovel human excrement between pits, while on the RPF.

Professor Stephen Kent wrote a paper about the RPF some 20 years ago,[82] but not one of the countries where the RPF is practiced has even investigated the use of these invidious labor camps. These camps exist in England, Denmark, Australia and the USA.

MISCAVIGE

Miscavige took power after Hubbard died. He was 14, when he joined the Sea Organization, and served as a cameraman when Hubbard was making instructional videos in the late 70s. In 1983, in a sworn declaration, Hubbard said "I wish to take this opportunity to communicate my unequivocal confidence in David Miscavige."[83] Hubbard died in 1986, Miscavige soon dislodged Hubbard's appointed successor, Pat Broeker, to become "Chairman of the Board".

Miscavige had overseen the restructuring of Scientology, in the early 1980s. The cult was separated into over 400 corporations, but it is clear that Miscavige has control over every Scientology entity, in spite of the complex web created during Hubbard's last years. By this time, Scientology had created a secret headquarters at Gilman Hot Springs, in California. This 500-acre property is surrounded by high wire and sensor pads, which make it impossible for staff to escape. Gilman has its own Rehabilitation Project Force.

Hubbard often had temper tantrums, which are called "severe reality adjustments" by Sea Organization members. He would rant and rave, humiliating any staff member who had irritated him, by standing inches away from them and bawling insults at the top of his voice. David Miscavige has a reputation for delivering these "severe reality adjustments", but is also known for physically attacking staff members. At one point, he rounded up all of the senior executives at Gilman Hot Springs and confined them to a double-trailer, called the hole, for months on end. It is possible that some executives spent years in this prison.[84]

Hubbard promised fifteen levels above OT VIII, but Miscavige has failed to find them. He believed that Hubbard's appointed successor, Pat Broeker, had the missing levels, so hired a private investigation team to spy on Broeker for 24 years, at a cost of over ten million dollars. As yet, the levels from OT IX to OT XXIII have not been found.

THE SCIENTOLOGIST

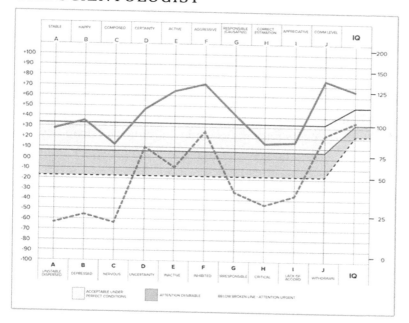

Few Scientologists have the full picture of Hubbard and his intentions. Most are even unaware that Scientology uses hypnotic techniques. Most Scientologists are well-intentioned, and believe that they are saving the world, or "Clearing the Planet" as Hubbard put it. Scientologists come from all walks of life, but, as with other cult groups, they tend to be well-educated and socially responsible. They want to change the world for the better, so justify their attack upon critics. Scientology has many rich patrons, who support the cult without a real awareness of its history or its objectives.

Scientology uses street recruiters who ask innocent survey questions, so that they can invite the recruit to take a "free personality test" at a Scientology center. The test is called the Oxford Capacity Analysis, but it has nothing to do with Oxford University, and was written by a merchant seaman with no training in psychology. It is a 200-question test, which asks for highly personal information. The recruit is not told that any high score will be marked down, on the basis that only a Scientologist could genuinely score well on such a test. The recruit - called a "prospect" - is told that the test shows problems that can be solved with a Scientology course. The recruiter will try to find the prospect's "ruin" - whatever is ruining the prospect's life - driving the person down emotionally with the fear that the condition will worsen. The training manual for recruiters says, "when you point out a low score … say "Scientology can handle that". No matter what the problem, the solution will usually be the Scientology Communication Course.

The Communication Course consists of a series of "training routines". In the first, the prospect sits silent and motionless, with eyes closed, in front of a "coach". This makes the prospect accept the environment and drop any defenses. In the second - TR-0 - the eyes are open, and the prospect and the coach "confront" each other, silently. This drill is done for "some hours", and will lead to hallucination, as will any fixed perception. It usually leads to a euphoric state, where colors seem brighter and the senses seem heightened. This state is familiar to all hypnotists, as a consequence of trance induction.

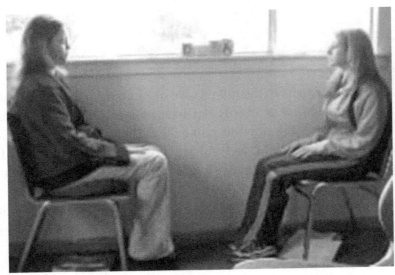

"TR-0" is followed by "TR-0 Bullbait", where the prospect is to sit silent and motionless, gazing at the coach, who tries to upset the prospect's concentration by making ridiculous or lewd comments. Once the prospect can sit without flinching, the pair move on to "TR-1", where passages are read at random from *Alice in Wonderland* by the prospect. "TR-2" teaches the prospect to acknowledge verbally any statement with *good, fine, thank-you,* or *alright.* "TR-3" teaches the repetition of a question in exactly the same words, until an answer is received. The final drill on the Communication

Course, "TR-4" is meant to teach the prospect not to be thrown off a question by anything the coach says or does.

Scientologists are well known for making fixed eye-contact. This maintains the altered state, in which they remain susceptible to the teachings. In nature, such "confronting" is employed by predators. Soldiers and police officers have long been trained in this dominance technique.

The new Scientologist may next be subjected to the original "Book One" techniques, which Hubbard withdrew because of their hypnotic nature, back in 1951.[85] They were reintroduced without comment or warning, in the late 1970s. In this original technique, the subject or "preclear" is age-regressed to relive past trauma. Hubbard explained that as they go into "reverie", preclears eyelids will flutter. He later pointed out that this is a sign of hypnotic trance, though Scientologists routinely declare that their methods are not hypnotic.

The "Purification Rundown" is another early stage of a Scientology career. This course has been declared fraudulent in France. During the Purification Rundown, subjects take increasing doses of vitamins and minerals, often leading to extraordinary amounts, many times above the recommended daily allowance. Several vitamins become toxic at high dosage. Subjects run until they are sweating and spend four or five hours a day in a hot sauna.

Such high levels of vitamins can create various physiological reactions, including drug-like experiences. Hubbard attributed these reactions to the removal of drugs and pollutants from the body. He even made the ridiculous claim that LSD lodges in fatty tissue. As LSD is both highly unstable and water soluble, this is impossible, but it shows Hubbard's usual scientific ignorance. There have been several deaths on the Purification Rundown. It may also permanently interfere with an individual's metabolism. Heat exhaustion is a frequent problem.

After the Purification Rundown, the "preclear" will undergo yet another hard-sell interview, and might well go onto the Hubbard Key to Life Course, for about $8000. This course supposedly undercuts all previous education by giving the individual the basics of literacy. Factually, because it treats all clients as pre-school children, it tends to cause age-regression and heighten an infantile, uncritical dependence on Scientology. From here the "preclear" will progress through the Hubbard Life Orientation Course and on to "objective processing", which uses a repetitive series of actions to induce euphoric states.

Where most groups have a handful of techniques to induce altered states, Scientology boasts over 2000. Many aim at "exteriorization" from the body. Scientologists believe that they can separate from their bodies and travel as spiritual beings or "thetans". More usually, they describe the effect known as "depersonalization", where they feel remote from their physical form, but have no external perception. This euphoric dissociation is often achieved. It can lead to severe accidents. I once spoke to a man who had walked through a plate glass window while "exterior", sustaining significant damage.

The "objective processes" are aimed at such "exteriorization". These procedures were introduced in the 1950s. Hubbard asserted that control must be taken by the counselor to show the "preclear" that his "reactive mind" can be controlled. In each "objective process", the individual is given strict and unvarying orders to repeat an overwhelmingly tedious cycle of behavior. In "Opening Procedure by Duplication", for example, a book is placed on a table at one end of a room, and a bottle on another, against the opposite wall. The Scientology "auditor" directs the "preclear" to look at the book, to walk over to it, to pick it up and to identify its temperature, color and weight. The procedure is repeated for the bottle. Sessions last for up to two hours and usually lead to dissociative euphoria and a sensation of floating, which Scientologists believe indicates that they are "exterior" from their bodies. These are actually typical hypnotic responses.

Scientology asserts that the writings of Ron Hubbard are all "scriptural". They must be followed exactly, as doctrine. This would include his attacks upon democracy and his support for "benign monarchy."[86] Hubbard believed that dictatorship is the best form of government.

Hubbard was also at odds with the equality of the sexes: "The historian can peg the point where a society begins its sharpest decline at the instant when women begin to take part, on an equal footing with men in political and business affairs." He was also markedly racist, boasting of his "Anglo-Saxon" form of therapy[87] and denying entirely any problems caused by Apartheid, in South Africa: "The problem of South Africa is different than the world thinks. There is no native problem ... the South African government is not a police state."[88]

His personal life reeks of hypocrisy. He was a man who abused and abandoned all three of his wives, yet claimed to be an expert on marriage. His son's suicide stands against his claim to expertise as a parent. Hubbard railed against homosexuality, even though he had gay sex himself.[89] His son, Quentin, committed suicide, after having gay sex. He killed himself, even though he had done every single step of his father's "Bridge to Total Freedom" - including the vaunted Class XII course, which remains the highest training for a Scientology "auditor".

Hubbard was a 120-cigarette a day user and a multiple drug abuser - by his own admission, in literature published by Scientology - whose "technology" is supposed to free addicts from addiction.

Hubbard promised total "self-determinism" to his followers and then had them sign contracts saying "I promise to uphold, forward and carry out Command Intention". Only after a *billion years* of servitude will they be allowed to actually become "self-determined", it seems.

THE PRICE OF FREEDOM

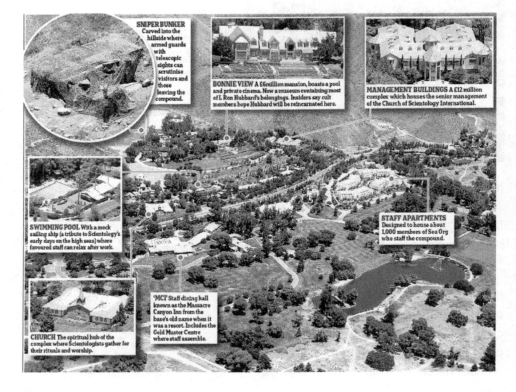

SNIPER BUNKER Carved into the hillside where armed guards with telescopic sights can scrutinise visitors and those leaving the compound.

BONNIE VIEW A £6million mansion, boasts a pool and private cinema. Now a museum containing most of L Ron Hubbard's belongings. Insiders say cult members hope Hubbard will be reincarnated here.

MANAGEMENT BUILDINGS A £12 million complex which houses the senior management of the Church of Scientology International.

SWIMMING POOL With a mock sailing ship (a tribute to Scientology's early days on the high seas) where favoured staff can relax after work.

STAFF APARTMENTS Designed to house about 1,000 members of Sea Org who staff the compound.

CHURCH The spiritual hub of the complex where Scientologists gather for their rituals and worship.

'MCI' Staff dining hall known as the Massacre Canyon Inn from the base's old name when it was a resort. Includes the Gold Muster Centre where staff assemble.

Scientology is notoriously expensive. While representatives of the cult will claim that it provides many inexpensive courses, internal materials show that these are simply bait for other extremely expensive "services". To complete all of the steps of the Scientology "Bridge" costs in the region of half a million dollars. Those who cannot afford the cost are recruited onto staff, often ending up in penury and working in substandard conditions in virtual slavery.

CELEBRITIES & PSYCHIATRY

The cult makes much of the adherence of celebrities - such as Tom Cruise and John Travolta - but makes no mention of those who have left, for instance, Nicole Kidman, Leonard Cohen, Van Morrison and double Oscar winner, Paul Haggis.[90] Tom Cruise has become notorious for his insistence that both cast and crew on his films should read Hubbard books and use Scientology procedures. A video of Cruise attacking psychiatry went viral on the Internet. Cruise seemed unbalanced. Cruise was following the "scripture" of Scientology, where Hubbard asserts that the "psychs" have been the enemies of humanity since the beginning of time. According to Hubbard, psychiatrists, psychologists and psychotherapists are in a conspiracy to enslave mankind. In an internal issue, Hubbard insisted that Scientology must destroy the "psychs" and take over "all forms of mental healing."[91]

let's sell these people

A Piece of Blue Sky

Hubbard, Dianetics and Scientology

Jon Atack

Asked for a comment about the new edition of my book, *Let's sell these people A Piece of Blue Sky*, long-term critic of Scientology, Arnie Lerma, wrote "Before there was the net, and before there was safety in numbers, there was Jon Atack." For a dozen years, I was a lone figure, publishing truthful information about the cult and helping hundreds of former members. I was subjected to daily harassment. My friends and family were contacted by private investigators; scurrilous pamphlets were distributed to every household in the town where I lived; protestors with placards marched in front of my house; and I was the subject of litigation both at home, in England, and in the USA.

With the development of the Internet and the World Wide Web, critics were able to make anonymous comments. Hundreds of web sites came into being, many of which are very well organized. In the past, dissenters would have to search public libraries, often finding that critical books had disappeared from the shelves - Portland library, in Oregon, reported that nine copies of my book were stolen during the first year of publication. Almost 200 copies have disappeared from UK libraries. Nowadays, it is possible for the curious to surf the net in the privacy of their own homes.

This has led to mass defections, during the last decade, including many senior Scientologists who are dissatisfied with the aggressive behavior of David Miscavige.

I left the Scientology fray in 1996. The cult continued to litigate against me for four more years. In 2012, I made my first public utterances about the cult for 16 years. I had become concerned that the majority of former Scientologists simply do not recover, without assistance. While the cult itself probably has only about 25,000 members, millions of people have received some form of Dianetic or Scientology "processing". Auditing can leave a set of positive suggestions functioning below consciousness. Unless Hubbard's ideas are challenged head on, they will continue to exert an influence. Once I have completed a recovery text for former members, I shall return to my work on the more general aspects of exploitative persuasion in our society.

THE FREE ZONE

From its inception, in 1950, there have been *hundreds* of Dianetic and Scientology splinter groups. Scientology has also influenced many other cult leaders, including EST founder Werner Erhard, Da Free John, Co-counseling founder, Harvey Jackins and Paul Twitchell of Eckankar. Independent groups have included Synergistics, Amprinistics, Dianology, Avatar, the Institute for Research into Metapsychology and the Free Zone.

None of the independent Scientology groups poses the same threat as the self-styled Church of Scientology, however, all use some if not all of the hypnotic techniques that form the core of Scientology, even when they have abandoned the harassment techniques of the mother cult.

The Free Zone was initiated by Captain Bill Robertson, a former member of a biker gang, who earned his sea captain's papers so that he could command one of Hubbard's vessels, in the 60s. Captain Bill believed that the world has been invaded by aliens from the Marcab system, as mentioned in a Hubbard lecture. He claimed that Transcendental Meditation was at the center of this invasion. In 1983, he said that there were already 200,000 Marcabians on Earth, disguised as human beings.

Bill Robertson died after he refused surgical intervention, believing that he could overcome a throat tumor through Scientology "auditing". Bill believed that he had been Hubbard's girlfriend, Astar Parmejian, 75 million years ago, at the time of the supposed OT III incident. In private, he dressed in women's clothes and acted out this fantasy. The Free Zone is among the largest independent Scientology groups, with thousands of members. It has proved especially popular in Russia and Germany.

SEA ORGANIZATION

FLAG CONDITIONS ORDER 6936   3 September 1982

BPI

SUPPRESSIVE GROUP DECLARE

"GALACTIC PATROL"

The group calling itself the "Galactic Patrol" is hereby labeled a Suppressive Group.

"Suppressive Groups are defined as those which seek to destroy Scientology or which specialize in injuring or killing persons or damaging their cases or which advocate suppression of Mankind." HCO PL 29 Jun 68 (Vol I, pg 484 OEC.)

The "Galactic Patrol" was formed by Bill Robertson, Dafna Robertson and Ernie Martin, all declared SPs, with the stated intention of pulling people away from the standard organizations of Scientology. The "Galactic Patrol" is apparently some off-beat mockery of the Sea Organization, based on the distorted view of the Whole Track as perceived by the above individuals. The group only serves to distract people from Standard Scientology and seems designed to restimulate others for the personal gain of the founding members.

Some people who have had connections with the few members of this group have already reported themselves to their Ethics Officer, recognizing the group for what it is. Any others who have had contact with this group or its members are encouraged to report the details of any such contact to an Ethics Officer or Sea Org Master-at-Arms.

HCO PL 29 Jun 68 ENROLLMENT IN SUPPRESSIVE GROUPS applies fully to this group. Specifically:

"Any person found to be connected to a Suppressive Group may not thereafter be enrolled in the Saint Hill Solo Audit Course or the Clearing Course."

In accordance with that same Policy Letter, no member of a suppressive group may ever be employed by any Church or Mission of Scientology, without special clearance.

The Church of Scientology is currently engaged in our most rapid period of expansion in history. All Scientologists are warned to not let these things distract us from keeping up with the increasing demands for standard Scientology.

POl Paul Laquerre
International Justice Chief
Authorized by AVC
for the
CHURCH OF SCIENTOLOGY
INTERNATIONAL

CSI:NM:PL:dr

Resources

In 1995, the editor of *The Village Voice*, Tony Ortega, learned about Scientology and decided to run a professional news web site about its activities. Despite constant harassment, Ortega continues to run his excellent *Underground Bunker* site. In Paris, journalist Jonny Jacobsen maintains the *Infinite Complacency* site. Arnie Lerma, Gerry Armstrong, Caroline Letkeman, Karin Spaink, Tilman Hausherr and Andreas Heldal Lund have all developed significant archives of Scientology related material on public websites. Solitary Trees is another of the many well-made sites that discuss specific issues with irrefutable Hubbard documentation. Steven Hassan's Freedom of Mind website and the Fight Against Coercive Tactics Network (FACTNet) site also contain relevant material.

The Anonymous movement has picketed Scientology organizations for some years. Scientology has become unfashionable, because of the availability of accurate information. In the Russian Federation, and throughout the territory of the Orthodox Church, much has been achieved by Professor Alexander Dvorkin, and our thanks are due to him for his exemplary work for more than two decades.

ABOUT THE AUTHOR

Jon Caven Atack was born in 1955, in Lichfield, an ancient cathedral city at the heart of England. As a teenager, he played drums in various rock bands. He is well known for his book, Let's Sell These People a Piece of Blue Sky, the first history of the dreadful Scientology cult. Jon studied art and had his first one-man show of paintings in London, in 1981. He is also known for his translation of the Tao Te Ching. Jon has four children and one grandchild and lives contentedly in a pleasant village, just outside Nottingham, where, in keeping with Voltaire's dictum, he tends his garden. He still plays drums, paints and writes.

[1] Hubbard had this to say in his pre-Scientology novel, *Fear*: "I have sought to show that demons and devils were invented to allow some cunning member of the tribe to gain control of his fellows." This is the lyric from one of the songs he wrote in his final years:" In olden days the populace was much afraid of demons/ And paid an awful sky high price to buy some priestly begones . . . Oh now here is the why that makes the world an evil circus/ No demons at all but just the easily erased evil purpose." from *The Road to Freedom*.

[2] Hubbard, HCOPL, *Principles of Money Management*, 9 March 1972R, Issue I, revised 4 August 1983, Finance Series 11R: "GOVERNING POLICY - The governing policy of Finance is to:

"A. MONEY.

"J. MAKE MONEY.

"K. MAKE MORE MONEY.

"L. MAKE OTHER PEOPLE PRODUCE SO AS TO MAKE MONEY."

[3] Flag Mission Order 375, reprinted 1992.

[4] International Management Bulletin No.108, 29 September 1987.

[5] HCO PL 26 September 1979, Issue III

[6] HCOB 29 September 1959, *The Organization of a PE Foundation*

[7] 13 May 1959, *Second Lecture on Clearing Methodology*, Organization Executive Course, 1991, p.18

[8] Hubbard, HCOB 17 March 1960, *Standardized Sessions*: "Dead-in-'is-'ead."

[9] Hubbard, HCOB 16 January 1968, *Starting of Preclears*: "All raw meat Preclears (on who has never had Scientology processing)".

[10] *PDC 20: Formative State of Scientology. Definition of Logic.*

[11] Hubbard, *What Your Fees Buy*, 1976.

[12] See Marc Headley *Blown for Good*; Jenna Miscavige Hill *Beyond Belief*; and Jefferson Hawkins *Counterfeit Dreams* for first hand accounts of Miscavige's behaviour.

[13] See Lawrence Wright, *Going Clear*.

[14] Land transfers, courtesy of the Montana Historical Society. For a detailed biography of Hubbard, see this author's *Let's sell these people A Piece of Blue Sky* and Russell Miller's *Bare-faced Messiah*.

[15] Hubbard, *Mission into Time*, 1973, p.4; *LRH's Autobiographical Notes for Peter Tomkins*, 6 June 1972.

[16] LA Times, June 1990.

[17] Albert Q Maisel, *Dianetics: Science or Hoax?*, *Look* magazine, 5 December 1950.

[18] Kima Douglas in the Armstrong case, 1984. Douglas, Hubbard's personal "Medical Officer" from 1975 to 1980 (Armstrong vol.25, p.4434-5), was asked by the Judge if Hubbard had any bullet wounds in his back. Her reply was succinct: "No, sir." (vol.25, p.4459).

[19] Hubbard, *My Philosophy*, 1965. Hubbard, PAB No. 124, 15 November 1957, *Communication and Isness*.

[20] Hubbard letter to Veterans Administration, 15 October 1947.

[21] Hubbard, "I know because I made myself a guinea pig on one of those experiments, and trying to get off a soporific was a tough job." He names phenobarbital as the soporific in the lecture. *Case Factors*, 15 June 1950,

Research & Discovery vol.1, p.124, first edition.

[22] http://www.gerryarmstrong.org/50grand/writings/ars/ars-2000-03-11.html

[23] Author's conversation with Jo Scott, 1984.

[24] Hubbard letter to Forest Ackerman, January 1949.

[25] Don Rogers personal communication to the author, 1984.

[26] Freud, Two Short Accounts of Psycho-Analysis, Penguin, London, 1962. See also this author's paper *Possible Origins for Dianetics and Scientology*.

[27] Grinker and Spiegel, *Men Under Stress*, McGraw Hill, US, 1st edition, 1945; 2nd edition, 1963.

[28] "It was claimed that through Dianetics the individual would be freed of psychoses and neuroses.[16] Amongst the "psychosomatic" conditions Dianetics claimed to cure were asthma, poor eyesight, color blindness, hearing deficiencies, stuttering, allergies, sinusitis, arthritis, high blood pressure, coronary trouble, dermatitis, ulcers, migraine, conjunctivitis, morning sickness, alcoholism and the common cold. Even tuberculosis would be alleviated. Dianetics would also have "a marked effect upon the extension of life." A Clear could do a computation which a "normal would do in half an hour, in ten or fifteen seconds." Hubbard claimed to have examined and treated 273 people and, through this research, found the "single and sole source of aberration." The book claimed that Dianetics was effective on anyone, who had not had "a large portion of his brain removed," or been "born with a grossly malformed nervous structure." Better yet, Dianetics could be practiced straight from the book with no training. Therapy would take anything from 30 to 1,200 hours, by which time the person would be Clear and thus free of all irrationality, and every psychosomatic ailment." Atack, *Let's sell these people A Piece of Blue Sky*, 2013, 2nd edition. *Dianetics; the Modern Science of Mental Health*, 1973 edition, pp.17, 51-2, 68, 92, 96, 156, 171, 181, 364, 392.

[29] "the other day an auditor performed a miracle the Pope himself would have been proud to own. A child had died, was dead, had been pronounced dead by a doctor, and the auditor ... brought the child to life." *The Scientologist: A Manual on The Dissemination of Material, Ability*, Major 1, 1955, ca.mid-March.

[30] Joseph Winter, MD, *A Doctor's Report on Dianetics*.

[31] For Hubbard's reliance on Crowley's *Magick in Theory and Practice*, see this author's *Possible Origins for Dianetics and Scientology*.

[32] Hubbard, *Conditions of Space Time Energy*, December 1952, *PDC* lecture 18.

[33] Crowley telegram to Karl Germer, 22 May 1946.

[34] The Crowley version of the "rosy cross" is found on the back of his tarot pack and in his *Book of Thoth*.

[35] Lloyd Eschbach in his autobiography, *Over My Shoulder*, remembered taking lunch with John Campbell and Ron Hubbard in 1949, when Hubbard made this statement. Fellow pulp author, Ryerson Johnson says that Hubbard told him, "The best way to make some money in this world is to play the God game."

[36] Hubbard to Helen O'Brien, 10 April 1952.

[37] Hubbard, in various lectures, recorded in Research & Discovery vol.1, pp.124, 305, 313; and vol.4, p.37. Also in *Dianetics: the Modern Science of Mental Health*: "Benzedrine [an amphetamine] and other commercial stimulants have been used with some success [to assist "reverie" in counselling]", p.363, p. 389 in later editions.

[38] Testimony of Hubbard's personal nurse, Kima Douglas, in CSC v. Armstrong, vol.25 (where she said that Hubbard had cut back to 4 packs a day in 1980) and Miller interview with Douglas. Douglas was Hubbard's personal Medical Officer from 1975 until her departure on January 16, 1980. From 1977 she was with Hubbard on a daily basis.

[39] see this author's paper, *Possible Origins for Dianetics and Scientology.*

[40] author's interview, in 1984, with Morley Glasier, the agent sent by Hubbard to steal from government offices in Rhodesia. Hubbard actually bought a hotel in Bimini, Rhodesia, intending to move his HQ there. He attempted to buy land in Malawi, with the intention of creating his own country.

[41] Auditor 41, 1968.

[42] Auditor 37, 1968.

[43] HCOPL 15 August 1967, issue I, OEC Vol.1, 1991 edition, *Discipline: SPs and Admin: How Statistics Crash.*

[44] Hubbard, *The Scientologist: A Manual on the Dissemination of Material, Ability,* Major 1, 1955, ca.mid-March. This is a vital document for an understanding of Hubbard.

[45] Hubbard, *Ron's Journal 1967.*

[46] In the UK, for instance, MP Clement Freud was assisted by Scientologist Margaret Butler. A former Scientology agent told me that she had sexually seduced another MP.

[47] This objective was not achieved, though the full extent of infiltration has never been revealed. The UK Home Office refused to investigate allegations against two Scientologists who worked under assumed names. Documentation for the Snow White project can be found at http://www.xenu.net/archive/go/ops/go732/go732.htm

[48] USA v. Mary Sue Hubbard, et al, Sentencing Memorandum of the United States of America, Criminal Case No. 78-401.

[49] Hubbard, Auditor 19, *OT and Beyond,* Auditor 19, 1966.

[50] Hubbard ("the Redhead") to his first wife ("Polly"), c. August 1938. Filed with the Library of Congress for copyright by Norman Starkey, where it is misdated 1939.

[51] Hubbard, *Overt Acts, Motivators and DEDs, June 1952, Technique 88.*

[52] Hubbard, *Scientology: A History of Man,* p.5.

[53] Hubbard, *Go Clear,* Advance! Magazine, issue 10, 1971; see also Hubbard, Auditor 231, 1988: "A Scientology CLEAR has: - Over 135 IQ - Creative imagination - Amazing vitality - Deep relaxation - Good Memory - Strong will power - Radiant health - Magnetic personality".

[54] Hubbard, *Keeping Scientology Working Series 1,* HCO PL, 7 February 1965, OEC vol.0 (1991 edition).

[55] Hubbard, *Notes on the Lectures.*

[56] Hubbard, *Assists,* Class VIII, taped lecture, 3 October 1968. "Also the Christian Church used (and uses) [hypnotic] implanting . . . These gangsters were the Nicomidians from Lower Egypt who were chased out for criminal practices (implanting officials). They took over the Nicene Creed before the year zero, invented Christ ... and implanted their way to power." Hubbard, HCOB 23 September 1968, *Confidential - Resistive Cases: Former Therapy.*

57 *Notes On Lectures given by L. Ron. Hubbard*, Phoenix 1954. This passage was excised when the book was reprinted as the Phoenix Lectures in 1968.

58 Hubbard, Professional Auditor's Bulletin 31, 1954.

59 Hubbard, *Modern Management Technology Defined*, from tape 5410C04.

60 Hubbard, HCOB 11 May 1963, *Routine 3: Heaven*

61 Hubbard letter to Helen O'Brien, 10 April 1953, *Dear Helen: Re Clinic, HAS*

62 Letter to this author from Don Rogers, 1984.

63 From this author's paper, *Never Believe a Hypnotist*: "Hubbard was also aware of the signs of trance: "a pre-clear after he closes his eyes will begin to flutter his eyelids. This a symptom of the very lightest level of hypnotic trance" (Science of Survival, book II, p.227); "A simple test is to watch the person's eyeballs. You will find as he lies there that the eyeballs under the closed eyelids will hunt back and forth. You can see the bump of them on the eyelids, and they will be wandering . . . the hunting indicates a hypnotic state" (Research & Discovery, vol.1, first edition, p.336); "The eye moving underneath the eyelid is the indication of when a person is lightly or deeply tranced. That is the second stage of which the fluttering eyelid is the first" (Research & Discovery, vol.3, first edition, p.94); The preclear's eyes will roll a little bit under the lids and when he returns, particularly, the eyelashes will flutter, which tells you immediately that he has become more suggestible than he ordinarily would be." (*ibid*); "Sometimes you will notice a tremble on the eyelids. This means the preclear has deepened his sense of sleep and has left some of his attention units somewhere. This is a very early stage of hypnosis. Be careful of such a patient. (Research & Discovery, vol.4, first edition, p.38)" The *current* use of the Hubbard Dianetics Auditor Course and the Hubbard Dianetics Seminar is in total contradiction to these admonitions. By returning to the 1950 method, Scientology has returned to direct trance induction. Both of these courses give: "When the preclear's eyes close and you notice his eyelids flicker, finish counting . . . " (p.54 and p.42 respectively, step two). These are not the only signs: "If the person begins to answer you literally . . . that means your preclear is now a hypnotic subject and you are running him in hypnosis." (Research & Discovery, vol.3, first edition, p.94; see also Research & Discovery, vol.1, p.336). These prohibitions form no part of any auditor training course known to this author.

64 Conversation with the author, 1993. Confirmed in 2014.

65 There is an oblique reference to this "experiment" by Hubbard in *Science of Survival*, book II, p.225.

66 For instance, Hubbard's 1953 book, *Scientology 8-8008*, which remains in print, lists 24 thinkers, from Anaxagoras to Plato, for "source material".

67 HCO PL 5 October 1971.

68 Hubbard's "marketing series" relies upon *Positioning: the Battle for your Mind,* by Reiss and Trout; Hubbard even published an annotated version of *Effective Public Relations*, by Cutlip and Center. Scientology "hard sell" procedures are based upon Les Dane's *Big League Sales Closing Techniques.*

69 Hubbard, Professional Auditor's Bulletin 13, *On Human Behavior.*

70 http://www.authenticscientology.org/page39.htm

71 For instance, see testimony by Walters in CSC v. Armstrong, vol.25, pp.4394-7; Kima Douglas, *ibid*, vol.25, p.4437; Nancy Dincalci, *ibid*, vol.20, pp.3530f; also Janie Peterson at the Clearwater Hearings, vol.4, p.81.

[72] HCOPL "Suppressive Acts - Suppression of Scientology and Scientologists - The Fair Game Law", 1 March 1965. In Church of Scientology of California v. Armstrong, Donna Reeve testified that "disconnection" had been used by Hubbard in the 1950s.

[73] See, for instance, Hubbard, HCO PL   1 May 65, *Staff Member Reports*, and Hubbard, HCO PL 22 Jul 82, Corr. & Reiss. 26.8.82, *Important Knowledge Reports*.

[74] In Flag Order 2191, 15 Nov 1969, Hubbard ordered harassment agents to read Curt Reiss's book, *Total Espionage*, which describes the Gestapo system.

[75] Hubbard, HCOB 23 June 1960, *Special Zone Plan: The Scientologist's Role in Life*.

[76] Hubbard HCO PL 15 August 1960, *Dept. of Govt. Affairs*. Also, ""If we do the above as our pattern, we will successfully bring the following <u>facts</u> into public consciousness: (a) People who attack Scientology are criminals. (b) That if one attacks Scientology he gets investigated for crimes. (c) If one does not attack Scientology, despite not being with it, one is safe." Hubbard, Executive Directive 149 International, 2 December 1966, *Branch 5 Project: Project Squirrel*. For a more thorough analysis of the Guardian's Office, see this author's *Let's sell these people A Piece of Blue Sky*. For an extended discussion of the cult's harassment techniques, see this author's paper, *Scientology: the Church of Hate - An Anti-Social Religion Emerges in the Space Age*.

[77] Casey Hill v Church of Scientology, Canadian Supreme Court, file no. 24216, 20 February and 20 July 1995.

[78] International Association of Scientologists "event", 2001.

[79] This is illustrated on the cover of the 1968 -1972 editions of Hubbard's Dianetics: the Evolution of a Science, which shows Loyal Officers loading boxes of "clusters" into the hold of a space ship. Elsewhere, Hubbard asserted that Xenu's followers were rebels, however, he also claimed that the Sea Org was mimicking the winning side in that supposed conflict.

[80] "An E-meter is better known as a "lie detector", Hubbard, HCOB 3 February 1960, *Security Checks*.

[81] Hubbard, HCOB 30 March 1960, *Interrogation*.

[82] see http://www.solitarytrees.net/pubs/skent/brain.htm

[83] Hubbard legal declaration, 15 May 1983.

[84] http://en.wikipedia.org/wiki/The_Hole_(Scientology)

[85] see above, note 63.

[86] "Adherents to all forms of ideology can be made to agree that "benign monarchy" is an excellent form of government", HCOB, *Politics*, 17 March 1969, Technical Bulletins, vol.6, p.317.

[87] "the only Anglo-Saxon development in the field of the mind and spirit," Hubbard, *Psychiatrists,* September 1955, *Technical Bulletins*, vol.2, p.267-9.

[88] Hubbard, HCOB 10 October 1960, *Current News*. See also the collection of racist comments at http://www.solitarytrees.net/racism/deny.htm

[89] The "ritual" to incarnate the Anti-Christ, with Jack Parsons, in 1946, is the OTO VIII ritual, which includes masturbation. Author Robert Heinlein revealed in his journals that he and Hubbard had sex together.

[90] Haggis's story is told in Lawrence Wright's *Going Clear: Scientology, Hollywood & the Prison of Belief*, Knopf, NY, 2013.

[91]Hubbard, HCOPL *Public Image*, 3 February 1969, Organizational Executive Course, vol.7, p.521; Sea Org Executive Directive 1890, 26 March 1969. See also Hubbard, *Confidential: Zones of Action*, Flag Order 1890, 26 March 1969 - http://www.american-buddha.com/cult.flagorder1890.htm